LIFE IN THE
MIDDLE
AGES

Mark Ormrod

Themes in History

The American Frontier
The Crusades
The French Revolution and Napoleon
Life in the Middle Ages
The Rise of Islam
The Roman Empire

Cover illustration: From the *Livre de Rustican*, a fifteenth-century French manuscript. Even in medieval towns, people often had large gardens and allotments for growing herbs and vegetables.

Opposite: The thirteenth-century court of King Alfonso X of Castile. Known as Alfonso the Wise, he was a great supporter of both artists and scientists.

First published in 1991 by
Wayland (Publishers) Limited
61 Western Road, Hove
East Sussex BN3 1JD, England

Series editor: Mike Hirst
Designer: Joyce Chester
Consultant: Rosemary Horrox, University of Cambridge.

British Library Cataloguing in Publication Data
Ormrod, Mark
Life in the Middle Ages. — (Themes in history).
I. Title   II. Series
940.1

ISBN 0 7502 0237 8

Typeset by Dorchester Typesetting Group Ltd
Printed and bound in Italy by
L.E.G.O. S.p.A., Vicenza

Contents

What Were the Middle Ages?

Historians describe the period of European history from 500 to 1500 as the 'Middle Ages'. The Middle Ages have this name because they took place between two other important periods in history. Before the middle period came the ancient history of the Greeks and Romans. After it came the Renaissance and Reformation, which marked the beginning of modern history.

The Middle Ages are usually divided into three stages: the early Middle Ages (often called the 'Dark Ages')

Right & Far Right *Two contrasting images of life in the Middle Ages. A leper is rejected by the wealthy, while knights joust at a tournament watched by fashionable men and women.*

(500–1000); the central Middle Ages (1000–1250); and the late Middle Ages (1250–1500). This book is about the central and late Middle Ages, so it covers around 500 years of European history.

Most of us have a picture of the Middle Ages in our minds. Some people think of the tales of Robin Hood, of knights in armour, of tournaments and castles. Other people think of a period of cruelty, persecution and superstition: we sometimes use the word 'medieval' to mean something that is old-fashioned or unfair.

A crusading army. Led by a priest, it includes knights and footsoldiers. The women and children are a reminder of the popularity of crusades; whole families sometimes took part in these expeditions to the Holy Land.

We must be careful to find the right balance between these two pictures. Most medieval people lived in conditions that we would find very hard to accept. Their homes were dirty, damp and cold, and they had none of the household gadgets that make our lives so easy today. Many children died at birth, and even those who grew up to be adults rarely lived beyond their thirties. On the other hand, we must also remember that medieval people had no idea of what our lives would be like around the year 2000. Their standards and expectations were very different from our own.

Europe must have seemed a much bigger place in the Middle Ages. Few people travelled more than a few kilometres within their own countries, let alone across the continent. Most people spoke in languages and local accents that could be understood only in their own regions. In fact, there were many more languages spoken in medieval Europe than there are today.

As the Middle Ages went on, Europeans began to learn more about other parts of the world. In the twelfth century they increased their contacts with Arab civilization and the religion of Islam. Many Europeans were hostile to the Muslims because they controlled the city of Jerusalem, an important centre for Christianity. European rulers launched crusades to defeat the Muslims and re-establish Christian control of the Holy Land. But some Europeans also appreciated the richness of Islamic civilization, and copied it in their own writings and art.

One practical problem in the Middle Ages was how to tell the time. During the day, sundials and hour-glasses were used, but they were not very reliable. At night, it was possible to tell the time from the movement of the stars. These instructions for telling the time were drawn up in a monastery in the eleventh century:

One of the first English medieval churches to have a clock was Salisbury Cathedral.

On Christmas Day, when you see the Twins lying, as it were, on the dormitory . . . prepare to ring the bell. And on 1 January, when the bright star in the knee of Artophilax is level with the space between the first and second windows of the dormitory . . . then go and light the candles.

In the later Middle Ages more and more people needed to know the time. About 1300 the first mechanical clocks were invented, probably in Italy. The building accounts of Windsor Castle for 1351–2 tell us what was needed to make one of the earliest clocks in England:

- **six pieces of timber bought for a certain clock in the great tower**
- **a great bell brought by water from Baynard's Castle [in London] to Windsor**
- **12,000 nails bought for work on the clock**
- **various pieces of iron and a hammer, total weight 72 kg, bought by Master Andrew the [clock]smith**

What do you think this clock looked like when it was finished?

Marco Polo arrives at Ormuz on the Persian Gulf. Western knowledge of the East was very limited; in this illustration the camels look more like horses, and notice the size of the elephant!

Later in the Middle Ages, people looked even further afield. In the thirteenth and fourteenth centuries, Christian missionaries and Italian merchants, such as Marco Polo, made contact with the Mongol civilization that ruled much of central and eastern Asia. In the fifteenth century, Spanish merchants began to search for a sea route to the Far East. Then, in 1492, Christopher Columbus set off across the Atlantic on one of these missions and discovered the vast new continent of America. Between 1000 and 1500, European people's knowledge of the world had been transformed.

The exploration of other continents and cultures is only one example of how medieval civilization developed and grew. The changes were often so slow that people did not notice them at the time. But if we look at the history of the period, we can understand how life altered during the Middle Ages. We can also begin to appreciate how much of the Middle Ages is still with us today.

Village Life

In the Middle Ages it was common to divide society into three groups:

- 'Those who pray': the clergy. Their special duty was to pray for all the Christians in their care.

- 'Those who fight': the nobility. They were professional soldiers who were expected to defend the people during times of war.

- 'Those who labour': the peasantry. They lived by the work of their hands and created the wealth that supported the other two groups.

This book illustration shows the three groups, or 'orders' of society. Top left, the clergy – notice the cardinals in their red hats. Top right, the nobility, who wear ermine, a kind of fur. Bottom right, the labourers, carrying the tools of their trades. The scene in the bottom left-hand corner shows the dedication of a book to the Duke de Berry.

The vast majority of people in the Middle Ages fell into the third group. In fact, in most parts of Europe, the peasantry made up over 90 per cent of the population.

Most medieval people lived in the countryside. Communities were usually very small. Anywhere with over 500 inhabitants would count as a large settlement. In some places, villages were thick on the ground, but there were also large areas in central, eastern and northern Europe with virtually no human settlement at all.

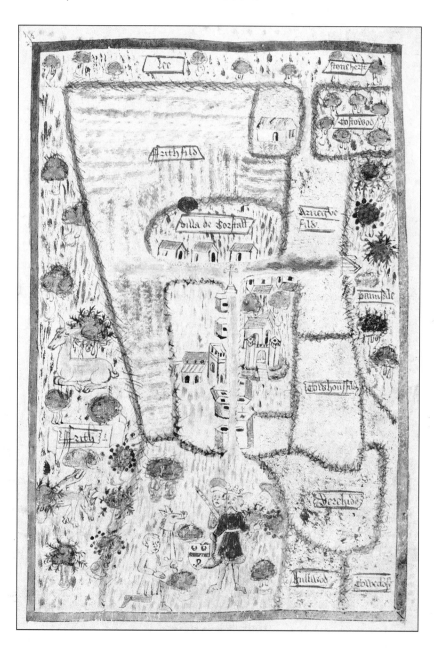

A late medieval map showing the village of Boarstall in Buckinghamshire. The village, with its market cross, church and manor house, is in the centre. Each of the open fields has its own name.

Most villages had a lord. Sometimes he was a powerful churchman, but usually he was a member of the nobility. In some villages, the lord lived locally in a castle or manor house. Often, however, he held many other lands and preferred to live in another part of the country.

The lord's estates were divided up into units called manors, which often consisted of single villages. The manor was run for the lord by an agent called a reeve, who was chosen from among the local peasants. Groups of manors were run by more important officials called stewards.

A large amount of the land on the manor was let out to the villagers, who paid the lord a rent. In many areas, the peasants' lands were not separated off with hedges or fences. Instead, there were two or three large or 'open' fields. Each field was split into strips, formed by the natural action of the plough, and each family was allowed a certain number of strips. This way everyone got some of the best land, and the peasants could share the responsibility for ploughing and harvesting.

Few places in Europe still have their medieval fields. A few long, thin strips of land survive in just one corner of this English village. Can you spot them on this aerial photograph?

Peasant farmers grew different crops in each field from year to year. Many farmers used a cycle of three years. One year a field might be planted with wheat, the next with oats, and in the third year it would be allowed to stand empty so that the soil could recover its natural goodness. Then the cycle would start again.

The most common crops were cereals (wheat, rye, barley and oats) and pulses (peas and beans). Potatoes were unknown in medieval Europe. Vegetables such as onions and cabbages were grown in the peasants' own gardens.

In mountainous areas, the peasantry depended less on crops and more on raising animals. Cattle were important because they produced meat and milk. Sheep were also valuable because they produced the wool from which almost all medieval clothing was made.

Some of the land on the manor was kept under the direct control of the lord: this was called the demesne (from which we get the modern word 'domain'). Besides paying rents for their own holdings, the peasants also had to do unpaid work on the demesne.

Not everyone did the same amount of work for the lord. Those who did most were the serfs. (In England they were often called villeins.) Serfs were subject to special controls. They were not allowed to leave the manor without the lord's permission, and they had to pay fines before their daughters were allowed to get married. When a serf died, his son had to pay the lord a death duty.

A woodsman killing a wild boar. In autumn, peasants often killed animals and salted the meat before the winter began.

Some peasants had houses and gardens in the village but did not rent land on the manor. They made their living as wage labourers. During the harvest season in August and September, they were often paid by the lord to help on the demesne. Peasant families with large holdings on the manor also used this casual labour force from time to time.

Many lords laid down strict rules about the work to be performed by their serfs. This list of services was drawn up for the serfs on the manor of Hinton in Suffolk in the thirteenth century. The manor was owned by Blythburgh Priory. The list tells us about the amount of work done in village communities at different times of the year. Notice how some of the dates were worked out according to religious festivals.

From Michaelmas [29 September] to the feast of St Augustine [26 May] the serfs shall plough the priory's land with their own ploughs, two men operating one plough for one day a week . . . During the same period they shall do manual labour one day a week from early morning until noon, except in the weeks of Christmas and Easter . . .

From the feast of St Augustine [26 May] to the feast of St Peter in Chains [1 August] they shall work one day each week from early morning till evening . . .

In the autumn [1 August to 29 September] they shall reap in the priory's fields four days a week . . .

How much time would the serfs have had left for working on their own lands in the village?

Medieval peasants going about their work: reaping, threshing corn and making wine. This stone carving decorates the church of St Denis in Paris.

Right *Medieval bee-keepers. Honey was used a great deal in the Middle Ages to sweeten food and drink.*

Above *A woman spinning wool on a distaff. This was a common task; the modern word 'spinster' comes from the medieval English word for a woman spinner.*

Women were very important in the village economy. During the central Middle Ages they tended to work at home, growing vegetables, keeping hens and geese, spinning wool, making butter and cheese, preparing food and looking after their children. Some women also ran businesses: most of the ale drunk in medieval villages was made by women brewers. In the late Middle Ages women began to do more work in the open fields.

Most peasant families lived in single-storey buildings, often with just one or two rooms. Their diet was extremely basic, and rarely changed. Almost all peasants ate porridge for breakfast. Their midday meal was mostly bread, perhaps with a small amount of cheese. In the evening, they usually ate pottage, a soup thickened with vegetables. Meat was a rare treat. Few peasant households had ovens, and all the cooking was done over an open fire. Bread was made at home, but had to be baked in the village oven which was owned by the lord.

Village life in the Middle Ages was routine and often very hard. But this did not stop peasants from having some fun. No work was done on Sundays, and there were many religious festivals to be celebrated throughout the year. Because the Christmas holiday fell at a time when little work could be done in the fields, it often lasted two weeks or more.

To a large extent, medieval civilization was built on the wealth that came out of the land. The peasants who worked that land were of great importance in the development of European history.

Kings, Nobles and Knights

The political map of medieval Europe was very different from how it looks today. Within the British Isles, Wales and Ireland were only gradually brought under English rule, and Scotland continued to be an independent country until 1603. In the Iberian peninsula there were several different kingdoms, including Portugal, Castile and Aragon. Germany, the Low Countries and northern Italy were divided

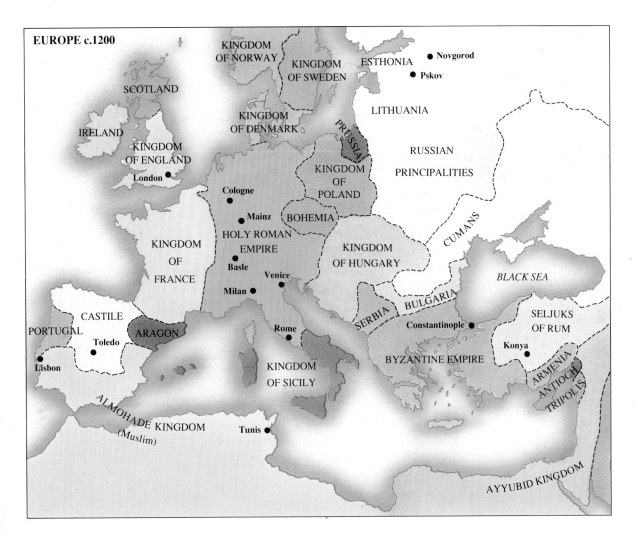

EUROPE c.1200

into hundreds of tiny states, many of them based around single cities. In theory, the Holy Roman Emperor was the overlord of Germany and Italy, but in practice his power was very limited.

The larger states of medieval Europe were ruled by kings. Kingship was looked upon as the best form of government because it was believed to have been approved by God. Most kings ruled by hereditary right: when one king died, he was succeeded by his eldest son. Queens were not normally allowed to rule in their own right, but as the wives and mothers of kings they were often powerful and played an important part in politics.

It was the duty of a king to defend his people from outside attack and to maintain law and order within his realm.

The coronation of Edward I of England. Edward's subjects saw him as the new King Arthur.

Some kings travelled around their lands, dealing in person with most of the business of government. However, in the late Middle Ages a lot of work was taken over by officials who found it easier to work in one place. As a result, London and Paris became recognized as the capital cities of England and France.

Kings were the heads of feudal society. The word 'feudalism' has been invented by historians to describe the way in which medieval society was organized. Kings and great lords gave pieces of land, called fiefs, to their followers, or vassals. In return, a vassal gave military support to his lord in times of war. The vassal would equip himself to fight as a knight, or cavalryman.

Feudalism grew up naturally in France in the tenth and eleventh centuries, and was imported into England by the Normans after 1066. William the Conqueror carved up his new kingdom to make large fiefs or baronies for his important followers. When Domesday Book (a survey of the kingdom) was compiled in 1086, about half of all the land in England was held by Norman barons. Over the next century they divided up their holdings to make smaller fiefs for their knights. By the end of the twelfth century the king of England could command the service of about 5,000 knights through this system.

Below *The life-sized sculpture of Edward, the Black Prince, from his tomb at Canterbury Cathedral. Like all the noblemen of his day, he was buried with full military honours.*

Left *A knight receives a sword from his lord. The sword was a symbol of the knight's importance and his role as a soldier. The sword was treated with great honour.*

RETVR:CASTELLVM:AT·HESTENGA CEASTRA

Building an early castle. It consisted of a mound of earth (or motte). On top was a wooden fence (palisade) or stone wall called a bailey. This scene comes from the Bayeux Tapestry, which tells the story of the Norman conquest of England in 1066.

The barons and their knights formed the nobility, the top level of medieval society. The highest-ranking nobles were the dukes, followed by the counts (known in England as earls). Noble titles were passed on from father to son: if a nobleman left only daughters, then the title died out, though the land was often divided between the surviving women of the family.

Some noblemen were very powerful. For example, the dukes of Burgundy, who started out as vassals of the king of France, built up an independent state in the late fourteenth and fifteenth centuries. Knights had much less wealth and influence, and sometimes controlled just one or two manors. But all the members of this class had three important things in common.

First, most nobles were involved in the army. Under normal circumstances only noblemen rode into battle on horseback. Horses and suits of armour cost a lot of money, and few peasants could afford such things. Equipment also became more expensive as time went on. In the central Middle Ages, knights wore simple helmets and tunics of chain mail; but in the late Middle Ages both knights and their horses began to wear armour made out of solid sheets of metal.

Right *Château Gaillard at Les Andelys in France, built by Richard I, King of England and Duke of Normandy, at the end of the twelfth century. It is perched on a high, rocky outcrop. Richard said that he could have defended it even if the walls had been made of butter!*

Left *Beaumaris Castle, one of a number of castles built by Edward I of England to defend his newly-conquered lands in Wales. Notice the symmetry of the design, the series of moats, the two ring-walls enclosing an outer and an inner bailey, and the huge keep at the centre.*

The second thing that brought the nobility together was their work in government. The most powerful noblemen acted as members of the royal council, advising the king on matters of state. The lesser nobility often helped in local government. England, for instance, was divided up into units called shires or counties, each of which was run by a sheriff. The sheriff was chosen from among the knights who lived in the relevant shire. Sheriffs had many duties: they made proclamations, brought criminals to justice, and helped collect taxes.

Right *A fortified manor house in Kent. The tower was built in the late fourteenth century, when the south coast of England was under attack from the French. The round tower and wide moat were the latest ideas in defence.*

Above *A medieval lord goes hunting. Hawks and falcons were prized possessions. Like hunting dogs, they were often treated as pets.*

The third thing that united the nobility was their lifestyle. Nobles were expected to avoid all forms of manual labour and were not supposed to take part in activities such as trade or banking. Instead, they were meant to live off the profits of their country estates and devote themselves to military training. For many nobles – women as well as men – life revolved around riding, hunting and hawking.

The house and household were important symbols of the nobility's power. The castle provided accommodation not only for the lord and his family, but also for the tens and sometimes even hundreds of servants – cooks, stable lads, laundry women or bodyguards – who made up the household of a great lord. Knights built much smaller residences, which are often called manor houses. But, like a castle, a manor house often included some form of fortification such as a moat or a tower. Usually the castle and manor house also had a large hall in which the family could entertain guests and followers.

The greatest divide in medieval society was that between lords and peasants. Kings and nobles lived lives that were completely different from the lives of most of their subjects. To the peasants, the nobility must have seemed as rich and exotic as film stars seem to us. What do you think medieval peasants thought about their lords?

Medieval kings and nobles devoted themselves to chivalry. The tournament was their most important social event. Groups of knights would meet to fight mock battles, either one-to-one or in large groups. This is an account of a tournament held by King Edward I of England in 1284:

The earls, barons and knights of the kingdom of England gathered together with many great men from overseas . . . for a Round Table proclaimed at Nefyn [in North Wales]. They joined in celebrations and tournaments to celebrate the king's recent victory over the Welsh.

The idea of a 'Round Table' came directly from the stories of the legendary British King Arthur. Edward I liked to think of himself as the new Arthur. Many of his subjects also liked this idea. After the king's death, a chronicler called Peter Langtoft wrote this verse:

**Of chivalry, after King Arthur, Was King Edward the flower of Christendom.
He was so handsome and great, so powerful in arms,
That of him may we speak as long as the world lasts.**

A knight equipped for jousting. Under his red and gold tunic he wears a complete suit of armour. Notice the vizor on his helmet, which he would pull down while fighting. His horse would also be wearing armour.

The Church

A woman taking communion from a priest. All Christians had to receive communion at least once a year.

Most people in medieval Europe believed in the same religion, and that was Christianity. People knew that other faiths existed: both Judaism and Islam had followers within western Europe. But all non-Christians were regarded as 'infidels' and treated with some suspicion. Jews were expelled from England in 1290 and were persecuted in certain parts of Europe during the fourteenth century.

The only official Church in western Europe was the Catholic Church based at Rome and headed by the Pope. Occasionally, people tried to set up alternative Churches: two important examples are the Cathars in twelfth-century France and the Lollards in fifteenth-century England. But most people believed that everyone should conform to one set of beliefs and ceremonies. Christians who opposed the Catholic Church were often treated very harshly.

The Catholic Church was run by the clergy. Many of them worked as priests in the parish churches. Almost every village had its own church, and the priest had considerable influence over the people. He could force them to attend church, and could have them punished by a special Church court if they refused. The priest could also collect a tithe, a tenth of all that the peasants had produced from the land in the course of one year.

Only certain men could become priests. Serfs were banned, as were the physically disabled, although this rule was sometimes relaxed. No women could become priests. Priests were also forbidden to marry.

Priests were appointed and controlled by bishops, the Church's equivalent of noblemen. They owned large, wealthy estates and had their headquarters in cathedrals. The cathedral was by far the largest building in any medieval city.

Many of the medieval clergy lived in special religious communities called abbeys or priories. They took vows promising to remain in their abbeys for the rest of their lives and to spend their time in prayer, study and manual labour.

Unlike the priesthood, this life was open to men and women alike: the men were called monks and the women nuns. Except in a few rare cases, all abbeys were single-sex communities. Like priests, monks and nuns were not allowed to marry or have children.

There were numerous different orders, or groups, of monks and nuns in the Middle Ages. The most important were the Benedictines, who wore black robes, and the Cistercians, who wore white ones. Benedictine monasteries were sometimes found in towns, but most medieval abbeys were in the countryside. The Cistercians deliberately settled in remote areas so that they would not be distracted from their prayers.

The monastic orders were very popular in the twelfth century, and many people gave money and land to the abbeys. In return, monks and nuns said prayers for the wealthy people who supported them. They also provided schools and hospitals which were sometimes open to people from outside the monasteries.

Above   *Although women could not become priests, they could become nuns. This nun wears a long black robe and an elaborate head-dress called a wimple.*

Left   *St Guthlac becoming a monk at Repton Abbey in England. The hair on top of his head was cut and then shaved; the bald patch, called a tonsure, was a symbol of his new life.*

Medieval monasteries were self-contained communities, each like a small town or village. The largest building in the abbey was the church, where the monks or nuns spent their time in prayer. On the south side of the church was a cloister, a large open area with covered walkways where people could sit and read. The cloister gave access to all the main rooms of the abbey. The chapter house was the meeting place of the community, and the refectory was the hall in which the community took its meals. Above the chapter house was the dormitory, or sleeping quarters. Some distance from the main complex of buildings was the infirmary, where the sick were cared for. Apart from the infirmary, the only place in the monastery that had any heating was the warming room, where a fire was kept going and the monks were allowed to sit.

The daily routine in the monastery was highly organized. There were seven services every day, and at special religious festivals there might be more. These services were quite short: most of them lasted for about fifteen minutes. But because they took place at regular intervals throughout the day, they were the dominating influence in the life of the monastery. In some orders, the monks and nuns even had to get up in the middle of the night for an eighth set of prayers.

Monasteries owned large amounts of land, and monks were supposed to set aside some time every day to work in the fields. The Benedictines had serfs and wage labourers to help them. The Cistercians had lay brothers and sisters. These people took vows like the monks and nuns, but they spent less time in church and more time at work on the abbey's farms and in the abbey kitchens.

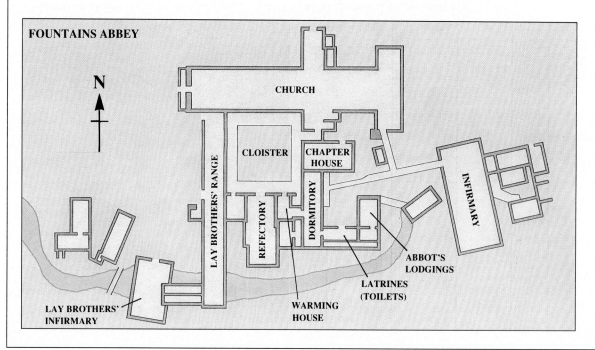

FOUNTAINS ABBEY

N

CHURCH

CLOISTER

CHAPTER HOUSE

LAY BROTHERS' RANGE

REFECTORY

DORMITORY

INFIRMARY

ABBOT'S LODGINGS

LATRINES (TOILETS)

LAY BROTHERS' INFIRMARY

WARMING HOUSE

The monks' and nuns' spare time was supposed to be spent in reading the Bible and studying books about religion. Some wealthy monasteries had large libraries. Every book was copied out by hand, and many were illuminated – illustrated with highly-coloured pictures and designs. The printing press was not introduced in Europe until about 1450 when a German, Johannes Gutenberg, succeeded in producing a printed Bible. It took a long time and great skill to produce a book in the Middle Ages. As a result, books were very expensive and their owners treated them as prized possessions.

Right *Monks in the choir of their abbey church, performing one of the services. Many of the services were sung to a type of music called plainsong. Can you tell which order these monks belonged to?*

Left *The ground plan of Fountains Abbey, a Cistercian monastery in the north of England.*

Right *The cellarer in a medieval monastery. He was responsible for supplying food and drink for the other monks. Here he pours beer from a barrel and tries some of it himself!*

Below *A medieval pilgrim carved in stone on the outside of Lincoln Cathedral. The hat and staff were often used to represent pilgrims in medieval art.*

In the thirteenth century a new type of religious group called the friars appeared. The word friar simply means 'brother'. The friars were like monks in that they took religious vows and lived in special communities. But unlike the monks and nuns, they left their priories every day in order to preach the Christian religion to ordinary people. The friars followed a strict rule of poverty, and had to beg for food, clothes and housing. They usually lived in towns. The two most important orders of friars were the Franciscans and the Dominicans.

Cathedrals and abbeys attracted large numbers of pilgrims. They travelled long distances to visit the famous cities of Europe and believed that their pilgrimages had a special religious significance. The cathedrals and abbeys had large collections of relics. These were bones, clothes or other items thought to have belonged to the saints of the Christian Church. People believed that if they visited the shrines that housed these relics, they were doing a good deed that would be rewarded by God. It was even thought that relics could work miracles.

The pilgrims who visited shrines were expected to donate some money to the church. The clergy used this money to improve and enlarge their buildings. Fashions in architecture were always changing, and the medieval clergy were keen to have examples of the newest styles.

Until the twelfth century, most European churches were built in the Romanesque style. The arches and windows in a Romanesque church are round, and the ceiling is made up of a continuous series of round arches called a barrel vault.

The cathedral at Santiago de Compostella in Spain, one of the most famous pilgrimage centres in medieval Europe. It is an excellent example of Romanesque architecture; can you see the round arches and the barrel vault? The chandelier and the altar date from a later period and are in a very different style.

Salisbury Cathedral in England, one of the most famous examples of Gothic architecture. Notice the pointed windows and arches, and the ornate decoration on the front of the building.

From the twelfth century, round arches and windows began to be replaced by pointed ones. This style of architecture is called Gothic. Gothic windows were decorated with tracery, stone carvings forming smaller shapes and patterns within the window space. The simple barrel vault also gave way to the more complicated rib vault, a series of interlocking pointed arches which created a star effect in the ceilings of churches.

The architects of medieval churches were highly skilled engineers. But the construction of a church was not just a technological achievement: it was also an act of religious faith. Christianity was a real and constant influence upon the people of medieval Europe.

Towns and Trade

Medieval towns and cities looked very different from their modern counterparts. There were hardly any really large cities. In 1300, Paris may have had as many as 200,000 inhabitants, and Florence about 100,000. But most towns were much smaller than this, with populations between 1,000 and 10,000 people (not much more than a large village today). Although most people who lived in towns were involved in industry or trade, many also kept animals and grew their own food. As a result, buildings were more spread out than they are today. On the fringes of many towns were large open spaces where the townspeople grazed their cattle.

Most towns in the Middle Ages had special political rights. The townspeople were granted charters by the king or a feudal lord, allowing them to appoint their own officials, collect their own taxes, and hold their own courts. Serfdom did not exist in these chartered towns; in theory many of the inhabitants participated in their own government. In practice, only a few of the wealthiest men in the towns had any real influence.

Medieval towns existed to serve the surrounding rural communities. Once a week – sometimes more frequently – the town would hold a market. Peasants could rent stalls where they sold any spare produce from their holdings on nearby manors. They then used their cash to buy goods that had been manufactured in the town and might not be available in their own villages: pots and pans, knives and tools, items of furniture, cloth and clothing and so on.

In addition to the weekly markets, some larger towns and cities also held fairs. These were much bigger occasions, drawing in traders from all over Europe. Fairs were held only once a year, but they could often last several weeks or even months. Kings, nobles and bishops sent their agents to the fairs to buy luxury goods: wine, spices, furs, silks and other fine cloth.

Builders working on a town wall. Many towns had fortifications so that they could defend themselves during wartime. Local taxes helped to pay for the upkeep of the walls.

Carcassonne in southern France. The town is surrounded by two circular walls with over fifty towers. They were restored in the nineteenth century, but Carcassonne still gives a good idea of what a medieval town looked like.

As the Middle Ages progressed and towns became more numerous, particular areas of Europe began to specialize in certain goods. The main business in many English towns was the manufacture of woollen cloth. The process of converting raw wool into finished cloth was long and complicated. One of the most difficult stages was fulling, when the woven cloth was pounded and washed in order to give it extra thickness. In the thirteenth century it became possible to do this by machine, using a water-powered fulling mill. The English could now produce a great deal more cloth.

Each stage in the manufacture of cloth was carried out by a different group of people: the spinners spun the raw wool, the weavers wove the cloth on hand-looms, the dyers coloured it, and so on. It took time and training to learn these skills, so craftsmen took on apprentices. Children became apprentices in their early teens and usually lived with their employers' families.

The people who co-ordinated the cloth trade and acted as wholesalers in this and other businesses were called merchants. Merchants needed large amounts of ready cash in

Medieval builders constructing a stone tower. Can you see the stonemasons' lodge in the distance, built of timber and thatch? Only rich people could afford to build with stone.

order to buy raw materials, to pay craftsmen, and to hire carts and ships for the transportation of finished goods. The wealthiest merchants often lent money to kings and nobles. In the thirteenth and fourteenth centuries, the merchant families of Florence, such as the Riccardi and the Bardi, created the first European banks.

Women were very important in medieval towns. They could be apprentices, could practise crafts, and in some cases were merchants in their own right. Since girls often married during or shortly after their apprenticeships, they were usually forced to give up their jobs and look after husbands and children. Nevertheless, some parts of the economy depended on female labour. Many shopkeepers and stallholders were women, as were a large number of silk-workers and embroiderers.

Medieval townspeople organized themselves into groups called guilds. There were many different types of guild within one town. The most important was the merchant guild, which was made up of wealthy wholesalers. It organized the markets and fairs. Then there were the craft guilds, each

There are very few figures available for medieval trade. The account books of merchants have mostly disappeared, and governments did not gather information about the economy. During the late Middle Ages, however, some kings began to charge taxes on imports and exports, called customs duties. The accounts drawn up by the collectors of customs in England still survive. They give us figures for the number of goods flowing in and out of the country.

One important export was woollen cloth. The customs officials worked out the customs payments on cloth according to its size and quality. The bar chart below shows how many broadcloths (the biggest and finest types of cloth) were exported from England at ten-year intervals between 1350 and 1500.

What do these figures tell us about the medieval English cloth trade? What sort of events would have affected foreign trade during the Middle Ages?

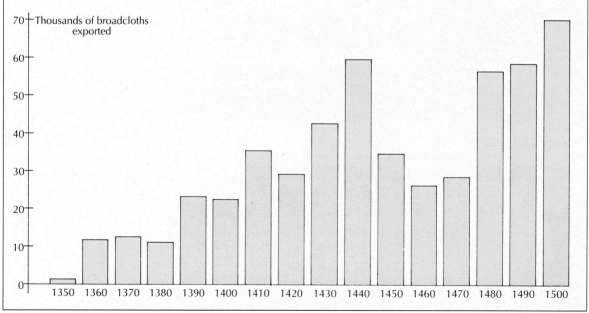

Thousands of broadcloths exported

of which protected the interests of one particular group of manufacturers: the weavers, the tailors, the cutlers, the goldsmiths, and so on. Finally, there were also religious guilds, which paid priests to say prayers for their members. They did a lot of charity work in the town. Women were usually

Left *A town house in Lincoln, built in the twelfth century. It belonged to a Jewish moneylender called Aaron. His customers included the kings of England and Scotland and a large number of monasteries. The carvings around the door and upper windows show this to be the house of a rich family.*

Below *Cologne was one of the most important cities in Europe during the central Middle Ages. After 900 it grew rapidly and soon spread beyond the original, Roman town walls.*

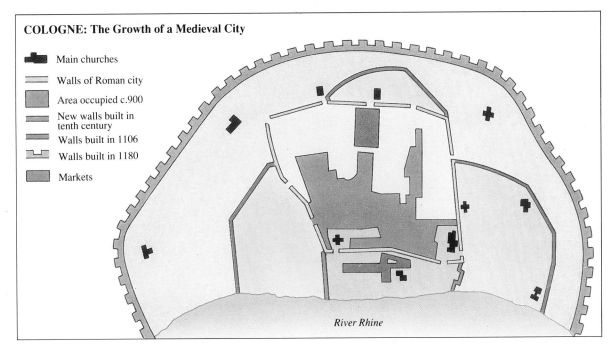

COLOGNE: The Growth of a Medieval City

- Main churches
- Walls of Roman city
- Area occupied c.900
- New walls built in tenth century
- Walls built in 1106
- Walls built in 1180
- Markets

River Rhine

The guildhall at Lavenham in Suffolk, built at the end of the Middle Ages out of the profits of the cloth trade. It stands in the centre of the town, and was the meeting place for one of the town's four guilds.

excluded from the trade guilds, but they played a very active part in the religious guilds.

The guilds were very important in the cultural life of the towns. They built churches, set up schools, and employed artists and musicians. Above all, they encouraged the development of drama. In June each year, the guilds in many of the larger towns would put on plays which told stories from the Bible. In the Middle Ages a person's trade or craft was often called their 'mystery'; so these pieces of medieval theatre are called 'mystery plays'. Some of the medieval mystery plays – especially those that tell the Christmas story – are still performed today.

Changes in Medieval Society

Many changes took place during the Middle Ages. The most important were to do with the size of the population. The years between 1000 and 1300 were ones of rapid growth: on a rough estimate, the European population went up from 25 million to 75 million during this time. The population grew so fast that by 1300 some parts of Europe were experiencing food shortages. Then, between 1315 and 1322, there was a series of disastrous harvests, and it was said that people even killed and ate their own children to stay alive. As many as 10 to 15 per cent of the population may have died from malnutrition during this famine.

Some of the biggest changes in medieval life were caused by the plague epidemic known as the Black Death, which ravaged Europe in the years after 1347.

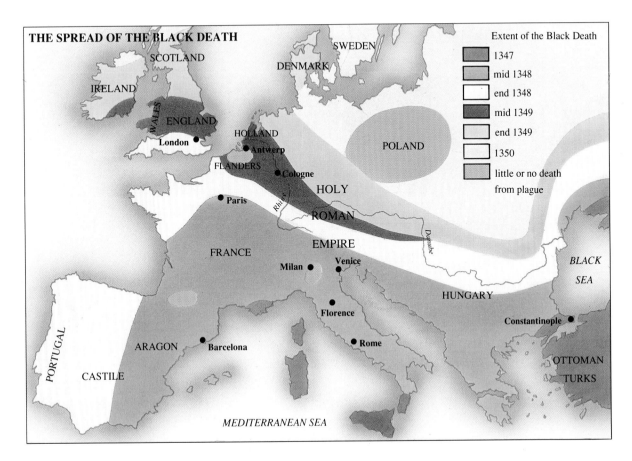

THE SPREAD OF THE BLACK DEATH

Extent of the Black Death
- 1347
- mid 1348
- end 1348
- mid 1349
- end 1349
- 1350
- little or no death from plague

By far the greatest shock came with the Black Death of 1347–50. This disease was probably bubonic plague. Plague is carried by fleas, which normally live on rats but which will feed on all warm-blooded animals, including human beings. The disease originated in the Far East, and was introduced to Europe by infected rats from a merchant ship in the harbour at Messina in Sicily. From there it spread to almost every part of Europe, including Scandinavia.

The Black Death killed about a third of the population of Europe – perhaps 25 million people – in less than three years. It was the greatest crisis that Europe has ever known. Many people believed that the Black Death was a punishment from God, and some even thought that the end of the world had come.

The plague returned at regular intervals over the next 350 years; it was not until the early eighteenth century that it completely disappeared from Europe. Although the later outbreaks of plague were less serious, they still affected the population. In England, for example, the population remained more or less the same throughout the fifteenth century because of the high death-rate from epidemic disease.

The Black Death affected every aspect of life. Whole communities were wiped out; in some parts of England, as many as 40 per cent of all villages disappeared between the fourteenth and the seventeenth centuries. Most of those that were left became much smaller.

A painting from a French church, showing the Black Death and its victims. The Black Death was often drawn as an arrow by medieval artists, because it struck quickly and without warning.

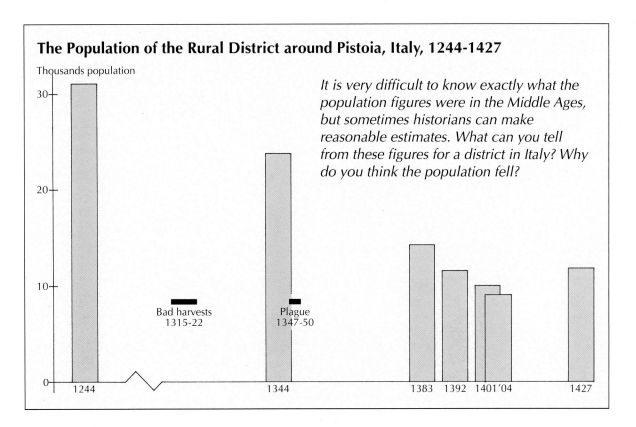

The Population of the Rural District around Pistoia, Italy, 1244-1427

Thousands population

It is very difficult to know exactly what the population figures were in the Middle Ages, but sometimes historians can make reasonable estimates. What can you tell from these figures for a district in Italy? Why do you think the population fell?

Bad harvests 1315-22

Plague 1347-50

1244   1344   1383 1392 1401 '04   1427

Lords now had problems finding enough tenants and workers to keep the manor going. One way to resolve this problem was to make the serfs work harder. Another was to keep down the wages demanded by casual workers employed on the demesne.

Many villagers resented their harsh treatment, and the second half of the fourteenth century saw an increasing number of disputes between lords and peasants. When the English government tried to enforce a controversial poll tax in 1381, some peasants protested about their conditions. There was an uprising called the Peasants' Revolt.

In the short term, the revolt of 1381 did not bring about many changes. But as the fifteenth century went on, people began to adjust to the new conditions brought about by the plague. Most peasants' standard of living improved. Lords now tended to lease out their own demesnes to new, tenant farmers. In England these prosperous peasant farmers became known as yeomen. Nor could the lords stop wages from rising, and by the middle of the fifteenth century labourers were earning twice as much as their ancestors had before the plague.

In 1381 a series of riots broke out in south-east England. Historians call this the Peasants' Revolt. Some of the rioters made their way to London to see the young king, Richard II. They wanted him to protect them from their lords and to reform the government. There are several accounts written by people who lived through the revolt. All the writers were members of the nobility or the clergy, and disapproved of what the peasants had done. This is what the monk Thomas Walsingham wrote about the behaviour of the rebels when they broke into the Tower of London on 14 June 1381:

Who would ever believe that such rustics would dare to enter the chamber of the king and of his mother with their filthy sticks; and, undeterred by any of the soldiers, to stroke the beards of several most noble knights with their uncouth and sordid hands? They talked in a familiar fashion with the soldiers . . . They arrogantly lay and sat on the king's bed, joking as they did so; and several even asked the king's mother to kiss them. The rebels, who had previously been lowly serfs, went in and out like lords; and swineherds set themselves above soldiers.

Do you think that this account is reliable historical evidence? Which words in the passage tell us what Thomas Walsingham thought about the peasants?

The Peasants' Revolt of 1381. King Richard II sailed down the River Thames to meet the rebels and hear their demands.

By the late Middle Ages, most English peasants were better housed, better clothed and better fed than their ancestors had been. Those who did not fall victim to the plague could also expect to live longer. In the fifteenth century, many people survived into their fifties or even sixties.

The biggest change of all came in the lives of women. The shortage of labour after the Black Death meant that women began to do many different kinds of work, particularly in the towns. The greater independence of women is shown by attitudes towards marriage. Before the plague most girls had husbands chosen for them, and girls from wealthy families were often engaged and married between the ages of twelve and fifteen. In the fifteenth century, many women did not get married until they were in their mid-twenties. They also had much more say in the decision about who would be their husband.

The late Middle Ages also saw important cultural changes. Many new schools and universities were founded in Europe, and more and more people received a formal education. The official language of the Catholic Church and of royal governments was Latin, but many people now learned to read in the languages they spoke every day, called the vernacular languages. There was a new demand for literature written in the vernacular; many authors began to write works in English, French, German, Spanish and Italian. Geoffrey Chaucer's *Canterbury Tales*, written just before 1400, is an important early work in English. About the same time the Lollards translated the whole of the Bible from Latin into English.

The growth of vernacular languages and literature also encouraged the development of nationalism. In the twelfth century few people in Europe thought of themselves as being English, French, Italian, and so on. Instead, they considered themselves to be inhabitants of a particular city or the subjects of a particular lord. But by the fifteenth century attitudes had changed. Kingdoms now had their own royal families, their own systems of government, their own patron saints and their own distinct cultures. In particular, the Hundred Years War between France and England (1337–1453) made people much more aware of the differences between their countries. By the end of the Middle Ages Europe already contained many of the different nations that make up the continent today.

Above *Geoffrey Chaucer, the author of the* Canterbury Tales.

Below *A battle during the Hundred Years War. The knights have dismounted from their horses and fight with their swords. Many battles ended in disorganized scrambles for booty and prisoners.*

The Medieval Inheritance

A medieval embroidery which depicts Saint Lawrence carrying the iron grid on which he was said to have been roasted to death. This needlework was done in England in the fifteenth century, and formed part of the robes of a priest.

The Middle Ages came to an end around 1500, when two important changes took place in Europe. The first was the Renaissance, a rebirth of learning and art, which began in Italy and spread quickly to all parts of the continent. The second was the Reformation, which challenged the power and authority of the Catholic Church by creating new Protestant Christian Churches.

The Renaissance and the Reformation changed people's attitudes to the way their ancestors had lived in the Middle Ages. In Protestant countries, people destroyed many of the shrines, statues and pictures that had been stored in the great cathedrals. King Henry VIII of England abolished all the abbeys and priories, and sold off their buildings and their lands. The monasteries fell into ruins. At the same time, nobles began to build comfortable new mansions for themselves and allowed their medieval castles and manor houses to decay.

There have been many other changes since 1500. During the French Revolution of 1789 many medieval documents kept by kings and nobles were deliberately destroyed. In England, the Agricultural Revolution of the eighteenth century created new methods of farming which altered the appearance of the countryside. In the nineteenth century, the Industrial Revolution meant that old towns expanded and new ones sprang up. In 1500 the vast majority of people had worked on the land, but by 1900 large numbers were working in factories.

During the Second World War (1939–45) many European cities were damaged by bombing. Medieval manuscripts and art treasures that had survived through the centuries were kept safe by being stored in caves, tunnels and cellars. But a number of medieval cities and many magnificent buildings, such as Cologne Cathedral in Germany and Coventry Cathedral in England, were almost completely destroyed.

Fortunately for us, there is still a great deal of material from which we can reconstruct a picture of life in the Middle Ages.

First, there is the written evidence. This includes chronicles, music and works of literature as well as the official documents kept by kings, nobles and bishops. The written evidence tells us a lot about the top levels of society. But because many records concerned the collection of taxes or the administration of manors, they can sometimes give us detailed knowledge about peasant families as well.

Castle Acre Priory in Norfolk. The monks were dismissed and the priory was destroyed during the Reformation. You can see the way in which the good-quality stone was stripped from the building, leaving only rubble in many places.

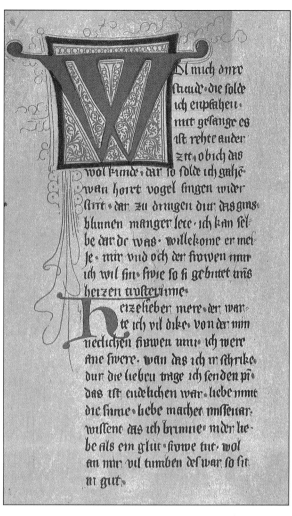

Left   *A medieval stained glass window from Canterbury Cathedral. In Protestant countries, a lot of stained glass was destroyed during the Reformation, though some of it survives in cathedrals and parish churches.*

Right   *A page from a Minnesinger manuscript. The Minnesinger were a group of medieval poets who wrote verses in the German language.*

Secondly, there are the buildings, the works of art and the personal possessions of medieval people. It is easy to spot some of this evidence: the ruins of many medieval castles and abbeys still stand, and most art galleries and museums have examples of medieval painting, stained glass, silverware, coins, and so on.

But there is much more to the medieval inheritance than books and buildings. Some parts of Europe still have kings and queens as heads of state. Many systems of government, both in Europe and elsewhere, are medieval in origin – think about the importance of counties in the British Isles and of sheriffs in the United States of America. Both the road layout and the street names of many European cities and towns give us clues about their medieval origins. In certain parts of Europe the landscape itself still bears the marks of the Middle Ages; in the countryside, you could look out for the pattern of ridges and furrows on the ground, formed by centuries of ploughing in the open fields.

Science and technology are becoming more and more important in helping us to reconstruct the history of the Middle Ages. Photographs taken from aeroplanes can sometimes reveal the outlines of deserted medieval settlements not easily noticed from ground level. Archaeologists can dig up these sites and find out about the housing, clothing and diet of the people who lived there. Even medieval rubbish can be analysed under the microscope: the things that people threw away tell us a lot about the way they lived!

Even if you live in a modern city far away from Europe, you can still find evidence of the Middle Ages at work around you. Think about the language you speak and the way it has developed out of the vernacular literature of medieval Europe. Look at nineteenth-century churches, railway stations and government offices. Many of them were built in the Gothic style of architecture. Why do you think it became so popular again? You could also look at some catalogues of furnishings, fabrics or wallpapers, and pick out the patterns that remind you of medieval styles.

The Middle Ages came to an end five hundred years ago – but their influence can still be felt in many different ways in our lives today.

Liverpool Street railway station in London, built during the reign of Queen Victoria. The Victorians thought the Gothic style of architecture was very dignified, and used it to honour their new invention, the steam engine.

One interesting archaeological dig took place at the remains of a medieval hospital at Soutra, near Edinburgh in Scotland. The waste pits at Soutra provide much evidence on medical practice in the Middle Ages. First, there are the herbs and other plants that were used to treat illnesses. Opium from poppies was used to calm patients; flax and hemp were both thought to be good for tumours or growths. Many other herbal remedies were used, and though they may seem strange to us, some of them had real healing qualities.

The other main deposit in the Soutra waste pits was human blood. This find is explained by the practice of 'bleeding', which was very popular in the Middle Ages. It was believed that a whole range of illnesses could be cured by deliberately opening up one of the body's main veins and allowing it to bleed for a limited period. If the amount of blood found at Soutra is anything to go by, then people were often drained of several pints before the flow was finally stopped. This practice can be very harmful; but modern medicine has shown that bleeding may also increase our resistance to infectious diseases. Thanks to the Soutra project, we now have a much better idea of medieval medicine and its effects.

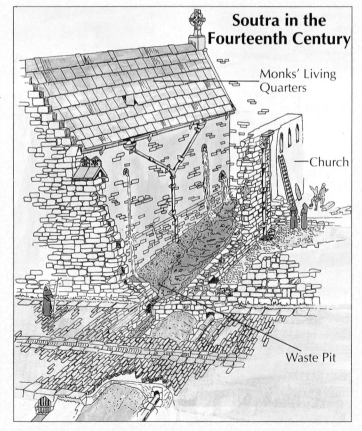

Soutra in the Fourteenth Century

Monks' Living Quarters

Church

Waste Pit

From their excavations, archaeologists have been able to reconstruct what Soutra must have looked like in the fourteenth century. There was a large open waste pit between the monastery church and the monks' living quarters. From there, waste drained away beneath the road outside the monastery. The remains from the Soutra pit have provided valuable evidence about how the monks treated illnesses in the Middle Ages.

Timeline

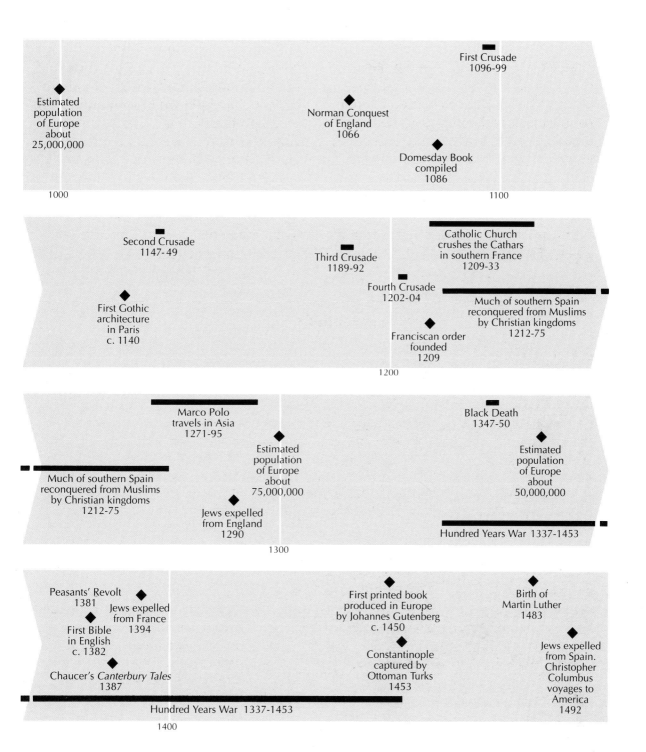

First Crusade
1096-99

Estimated
population
of Europe
about
25,000,000

Norman Conquest
of England
1066

Domesday Book
compiled
1086

1000

1100

Second Crusade
1147-49

Third Crusade
1189-92

Catholic Church
crushes the Cathars
in southern France
1209-33

Fourth Crusade
1202-04

Much of southern Spain
reconquered from Muslims
by Christian kingdoms
1212-75

First Gothic
architecture
in Paris
c. 1140

Franciscan order
founded
1209

1200

Marco Polo
travels in Asia
1271-95

Black Death
1347-50

Estimated
population
of Europe
about
75,000,000

Estimated
population
of Europe
about
50,000,000

Much of southern Spain
reconquered from Muslims
by Christian kingdoms
1212-75

Jews expelled
from England
1290

Hundred Years War 1337-1453

1300

Peasants' Revolt
1381

Jews expelled
from France
1394

First Bible
in English
c. 1382

First printed book
produced in Europe
by Johannes Gutenberg
c. 1450

Birth of
Martin Luther
1483

Jews expelled
from Spain.
Christopher
Columbus
voyages to
America
1492

Chaucer's *Canterbury Tales*
1387

Constantinople
captured by
Ottoman Turks
1453

Hundred Years War 1337-1453

1400

Glossary

Benedictines Monks and nuns who followed the Rule of St Benedict, a set of instructions written in the sixth century. Sometimes called Black Monks because of the colour of their robes.

Broadcloth A kind of cloth produced in medieval England.

Castle A fortified residence that was both a home for a lord and his family and a fortress into which the tenants on the manor could retreat during wartime.

Cathars A group of heretics who lived in southern France and northern Italy in the twelfth century. They believed in two gods: one good and one bad.

Chivalry The laws of war observed by medieval knights. Chivalry is also used as a more general term to express the ways of behaviour that all members of the nobility were expected to follow.

Cistercians Monks and nuns who followed a set of monastic rules first laid down at the monastery of Cîteaux in France in the early twelfth century. Sometimes called White Monks, from the colour of their robes.

Crusades A series of wars launched by Europeans against the Arabs to establish Christian rule in the Muslim-controlled territory of the Holy Land. The First Crusade began in 1095, and they went on for most of the central Middle Ages.

Demesne The strips of land (sometimes separate fields) on the manor that were kept under the direct control of the lord. This land was usually worked by serfs.

Domesday Book A survey of all the manors in England listed under the names of their lords. It was compiled on the instruction of William the Conqueror and drawn up in 1086.

Dominicans The friars who followed a set of rules drawn up by St Dominic of Ostia in the early thirteenth century. Often called Blackfriars, from the colour of their robes.

Feudalism A system of sharing out land. In theory, the king owned most land, but he granted territory to his barons in return for military service. The barons then granted smaller pieces of land to their followers.

Fief A piece of land given by a powerful nobleman to a knight in return for military service.

Franciscans The friars who followed a set of rules drawn up by St Francis of Assisi in the early thirteenth century. Often called Greyfriars from the colour of their robes.

Gothic The architectural style that was common in most parts of Europe between 1150 and 1500. You can recognize Gothic architecture by pointed arches, elaborate window tracery and rib vaults.

Guild A professional, trade or religious association.

Knight A medieval cavalry officer and member of the nobility.

Lollards The nickname for the followers of John Wyclif in late medieval England. They translated the Bible into English and disliked some of the beliefs of the Catholic Church.

Manor A block of land under the control of one lord and his agent. Many manors were made up of a single village.

Mongols A racial group from Mongolia. Under a series of powerful warlords, they extended their power across central and eastern Asia in the thirteenth and fourteenth centuries.

Open field A large field (normally of several hundred hectares) divided up into a series of strips. Each strip was allocated to particular peasant families, but the whole field was planted with the same crop and was often ploughed and harvested communally.

Poll tax A tax on each member of the population (rather than a tax on land or houses). It is often charged at a flat rate.

Protestant The Churches which developed in sixteenth-century Europe. They rejected the Catholic tradition of the Middle Ages in favour of a new or 'reformed' style of Christian worship.

Reeve The official who ran the manor on behalf of the lord.

Romanesque The form of architecture used in most parts of Europe from the early Middle Ages to about 1150. You can tell Romanesque architecture by the round arches and barrel vaults.

Sheriff An important public official in medieval England, appointed by the king to run the shire or county.

Steward The official who co-ordinated a series of manors on behalf of a powerful nobleman or monastery.

Tithe A tenth of all agricultural produce, payable to the parish priest.

Vault The ceiling of a medieval church, made up of a series of arches put together to make a continuous tunnel (a barrel vault) or series of star-shaped patterns (a rib vault).

Books to Read

There are many books you can read to find out more about the Middle Ages. Among the easier books, you could try:

J. F. Aylett, *In Search of History, 1066–1485* (Edward Arnold, 1983)

Mike Corbishley, *The Middle Ages* (Facts on File, 1990)

Stewart Ross, *Spotlight on Medieval Europe* (Wayland, 1986)

All of these contain many illustrations and are packed with information. Aylett's book is about England; the others are more general.

The following books are more detailed:

George Holmes, ed., *The Oxford Illustrated History of Medieval Europe* (Oxford University Press, 1988)

Edmund King, *Medieval England* (Phaidon, 1988)

Colin Platt, *The Atlas of Medieval Man* (Macmillan, 1979)

These books are mainly for adults, but they are well-written and have lots of good illustrations. Platt's book covers not just England or Europe, but the whole medieval world!

Index

Picture Acknowledgements

Aerofilms 11; Buckinghamshire County Record Office 10; CM Dixon 13, 20 (left), 22, 26 (bottom); Mary Evans Picture Library 23 (top), 38, 42 (right); Michael Holford 3, 7, 16, 18, 20 (right), 34, 40, 41, 42 (left); Billie Love 8, 14 (left), 17 (right); Mansell Picture Library 14 (right), 39 (top); Ronald Sheridan 36; ZEFA 30. All other illustrations are held by the Wayland Picture Library. The artwork on pages 15, 24, 33 and 35 is by Peter Bull. The artwork on pages 32, 37 and 45 is by Joyce Chester.

The author and publisher would also like to thank Brian Moffat of the Soutra Hospital Archaeoethnopharmacological Research Project (SHARP), 36 Hawthornvale, Edinburgh, for his help with the illustration on page 45.